A Gift To:

_____

From:

_____

On:

_____

HAPPY HOLIDAYS!

*Gifts of time and love
are surely the basic ingredients of a truly
merry Christmas.*

Peg Bracken

Grandpa's Christmas Tales

And Favorite Quotes

J.J. Turner, Ph.D.

PUBLISHED BY:

Solutions 2.0, Inc.
140 Monroe Drive
McDonough, GA 30252
678-296-1448

PRICE: $9.95 plus $3.50 postage and handling

May also be ordered from: amazon.com
www.jeremiahinstitute.com

INTRODUCTION

As a qualified Senior Citizen, Grandpa, and over 55, I want to affirm that I still *believe* in Christmas. It is my favorite time of the year. I also *believe* in Santa, the little old fat man dressed in a red suit; he is a metaphor of giving and love

I have taken a trip back to my boyhood and walked down memory lane relative to things I remember about Christmas growing up as a boy in Clayton County, Georgia. In the metropolitan areas of Jonesboro, Morrow, Ellenwood, and Rex. The reason I have written these little poems about my memories, is for my grandchildren: Gabriel, Anabel, Eliza, and Amelia; as well as for my siblings: Reba, Micky and Ricky, and anyone else who might care to know.

And special thanks to my Isabel for many great Christmases.

Why did I choose a poetic structure? Well, because I love poetry and I loved the challenge of finding rhymes. Also, it challenged me to put long stories in a brief poetic form; hopefully, for better reading.

I have also included some of my favorite quotes about Christmas. I hope you enjoy them as much as I do.

I know everyone has Christmas stories, and I encourage you to take time to jot yours down. It is a piece of history future generations will cherish.

HAPPY HOLIDAYS

J.J. Turner
Christmas, 2011

5

GIVE LOVE FOR CHRISTMAS

We are all making lists to buy special gifts
We could give more than a gift from a store
I know we can give so much more
This year let's give love on Christmas Day
I know there's no greater gift than love
Even the man who has everything
Would be so happy if we would bring
Him love on Christmas day
And every child on Santa's knee
Has room for love underneath his tree
Give love for Christmas on Christmas Day.

--Author Unknown

SPOTTING THE CHRISTMAS TREE

I was always impressed
When Christmas time came around,
Cause Daddy knew exactly where
A prize tree could be found.

A few months before Christmas
Daddy would spy the prize tree
And keep an eagle eye on it
Cause it would be free.

I never knew that people back then
Paid money for Christmas trees
Cause all the neighbor land owners
Let you cut them for free.

Sometimes the trees would
Have a few obvious flaws
But that didn't matter
To us and old Santa Claus.

I have always thought of Christmas time, when it has come round, as a good time; a kind, forgiving, charitable time; the only time I know of, in the long calendar of the year, when men and women seem by one consent to open their shut-up hearts freely, and to think of people below them as if they really were fellow passengers to the grave, and not another race of creature bound on other journeys.

Charles Dickens

CHRISTMAS TREE HUNTING

I must have been no
More than three or four
When Daddy and I
Went into the woods to explore.

Mama had bundled me with care
Cause cold and rain filled the air;
Daddy knew there was a tree,
And that soon I would get to see.

Just when I began to doubt
Daddy pointed to it with a smile;
There is stood shapely and tall,
The most beautiful Christmas tree of all.

Daddy had brought his handsaw
To cut the prize cedar down;
In a few quick minutes it was down;
I felt happy when it hit the ground.

Happy, happy Christmas, that can win us back to the delusions of our childish days; that can recall to the old man the pleasures of his youth; that can transport the sailor and the traveler, thousands of miles away, back to his own fireside and his quiet home!
Charles Dickens—*The Pickwick Papers, 1836*

DECORATING THE CHRISTMAS TREE

Once the tree was nailed
On a 2x4 wooden stand
We all were excited
As the decorating began.

There were no fancy blinking lights
Or exotic, colorful ornaments;
Just green, red and white paper ropes
That had cost only a few cents.

One string of large bulbs
Had to cover the whole tree
As the tree set in the window
For all our neighbors to see.

The most exciting moment
In decorating our prize tree
Was the placing of ice sickles
That sparkled with glee.

I have seen scores of trees
That have cost large amounts,
But none were as beautiful
As those that were free.

Instead of being a time of unusual behavior, Christmas is perhaps the only time in the year when people can obey their natural impulses and express their true sentiments without feeling self-conscious and, perhaps, foolish. Christmas, in short, is about the only change a man has to be himself.
Francis C. Farley

THE COST OF CHRISTMAS

One of the things I
Wasn't too sure about
Was why Daddy had to pay for toys
To help Santa Claus out.

Daddy said toys cost money
And Santa had expenses to pay
So it was only right
To help Santa pay his bills on Christmas day.

Daddy went to some loan company
To borrow for Christmas each year;
He did so with great joy,
Paying for it the rest of the year.

Back in those good old days
We didn't have a lot
So on every Christmas day
We were thankful for what we got.

When we were children we were grateful to those who filled our stockings at Christmas time. Why are we not grateful to God for filling our stockings with legs?

G.K. Chesterton

I wish we could put up some of the Christmas spirit in jars and open a jar of it every month.

Harlan Miller

SANTA CLAUS

It was almost impossible to
Fall asleep while tossing in bed
Just lying there excited waiting
For the sound of Santa's sled.

Drifting in and out of sleep
Listening for the reindeer hoofs;
I knew without a doubt
I would hear them on our roof.

The cookies and milk
Would be eaten by Santa Claus;
He would take time in our house
To stop for a refreshment pause.

So I have never doubted
If Santa Claus is real;
Each year at Christmas time
I know how I feel—he's real.

I heard the bells on Christmas Day
Their old, familiar carols play,
And wild and sweet
The words repeat
Of peace on earth, good-will to men!
Henry Wadsworth Longfellow

CHRISTMAS STOCKINGS

It was always exciting
To take my Christmas stocking down
There was fruit and nuts;
At the bottom a toy was found

The red Christmas stocking
Was an extra Christmas treat;
It was way too big
To wear on my feet.

It was the same red stocking
That was hung year after year;
It has a special place in my heart;
It's a memory I hold very dear.

Even now as a grandpa
I hang my red stocking for Christmas day;
I feel like a child again;
Excited about goodies that'll come my way.

Were I a philosopher, I should write a philosophy of toys,
Showing that nothing else in life need be taken seriously,
And that Christmas Day in the company of children
Is one of the few occasions on which men
Become entirely alive.

Robert Lynd

THE MEANING OF CHRISTMAS

Christmas is about more than gifts
Or a time to have fun;
It is a reminder of what
Our precious Savior has done.

Christ left heaven and came to earth
At this time we remember His birth;
It doesn't matter which calendar day
Christ has come to show us the way.

The story of the manger is sad
If we don't know the rest of the story,
About His victory over the grave
And ascension back to glory.

So regardless of your view of His birth
Let's all pause at this time
To praise our Lord and Savior
For coming to dwell on earth.

At Christmas-tide the open hand
Scatters its beauty o'er sea and land,
And none are left to grieve alone,
For love is heaven and claims its own.

Margaret Elizabeth Sanger

The earth has grown old with its burden of care,
But at Christmas it always is young....

Phillips Brooks

A WORLD WITHOUT CHRISTMAS

Do we dare to imagine
A world without Christmas,
No special season of cheer
Or a Savior to hold dear?

Can you imagine a
Child without that special day
No magic of Santa
With gifts or toys to play?

How sad the world would be
With Christmas magic gone:
Just the same old routines
No lights or trees in homes.

No thank you Mr. Scrooge
I'll not join you today;
As long as I am alive
I'll celebrate Christmas day.

Whatever else be lost among the years,
Let us keep Christmas still a shining thing;
Whatever doubts assail us, or what fears,
Let us hold close one day, remembering
Its poignant meaning for the hearts of men.
Let us get back to a childlike faith again.

Grace Noll Crowell

I BELIEVE IN SANTA CLAUS

There are some skeptics who don't believe
In the little fat whiskered man,
But let me tell you my friend
By old Santa Claus I'll always stand.

In a world of stress and pain
Where for many, Might makes right;
We need a kind friend to come
Down our chimney on Christmas night.

It is with a child-like faith
I choose to enjoy these holidays
No negative thinkers or unbelievers
Are going to take away my faith.

So when you see a smile on my face
Know I am in a blessed state;
It's Christmas time once again;
I'm enjoying it with family and friends.

Love came down at Christmas
Love all lovely, Love Divine;
Love was born at Christmas;
Star and angels gave the sign.

Christina Rossetti

Christmas is a day of meaning and traditions,
A special day spent in the warm circle
Of family and friends.

Margaret Thatcher

THE CHRISTMAS I GOT MY BIKE

There was one Christmas prize
Every boy longed to receive;
With the time approaching;
I became anxious on Christmas Eve.

At the mature age of eight
In just two months I'd be nine
I knew it was time
For that '26 inch bike to be mine.

I'm not sure I slept at all
With thoughts of that bike in my head
I could hardly wait for morning to come
And the time I'd jump out of bed.

Finally, the time had arrived,
But where was my bike?
It wasn't under the Christmas tree
Had old Santa forgotten about me?

Daddy told me to look out the window;
My bike was in the trunk of his car.
Santa had left it there because he came late
And he knew that I was still awake.

"

Twas the night before Christmas,
When all through the house
Not a creature was stirring—
Not even a mouse.
The stockings were hung
By the chimney with care,
In hopes that St Nicholas
Would soon be there.

Clement Clarke Moore

MY FOOTBALL SUIT

Like most boys of seven,
I had visions of playing football
So for Christmas I asked Santa for a football suit:
Shoulder pads, helmet and a regulation football.

As I dashed to take it from under the tree
I dressed like a pro for all to see;
There was only one major problem;
There were no boys with football suits to play with me.

I wore my suit with professional pride
My love for football I couldn't hide;
But soon I lost my football desire
And from the sport I did retire.

Christmas gift suggestions:
To your enemy, forgiveness;
To an opponent, tolerance;
To a friend, your heart;
To a customer, service;
To all, charity;
To every child, a good example
To yourself, respect.

Oren Arnold

MY RED RYDER BB GUN

Every boy raised in the country
Knew he had to have one;
It was a right of passage
To have a Red Ryder BB gun.

My time finally came to own that prized gun
There it was in a box under the tree;
As I loaded it with BBs, Mama warned me
If I shot my eye out I couldn't see.

As an armed hunter I sought for game;
Shooting tin cans and playing make-believe
I came upon a flock of black birds on a power line
I took aim and watched them fly into the trees.

I will not tell you about all the exploits
I had with my Red Ryder BB gun
All I can dare to say is
I wish every boy had one.

I'm dreaming of a white Christmas,
Just like the ones I used to know,
Where the tree tops glisten
And children listen
To hear sleigh bells in the snow....

Irving Berlin

He who has not Christmas in his heart will
Never find it under a tree.

Roy L. Smith

CHRISTMAS MUSIC

Christmas music was as important Santa Claus
When it came to celebrating that special time
Everybody loved Bing Crosby's White Christmas;
And longed for snow during Christmas time.

In Elementary School we'd have Christmas plays
In one I played a helping Elf singing a song;
Jingle Bells was always a favorite;
One time I got some of the words wrong.

On the radio in our home
Silent Night was a popular song
And when they played Rudolph The Red Nose Reindeer
We would all sing along.

The best of all gifts around any Christmas tree:
The presence of a happy family
All wrapped up in each other.

Burton Hillis

Christmas waves a magic wand over the world,
And behold, everything is softer and more beautiful.

Norman Vincent Peale

CHRIST IN CHRISTMAS

When I was a boy, around Christmas time,
There was major emphasis on baby Jesus
He was God's only Son
Who came to earth to save us.

In school, businesses and in homes
The manger scene was on display;
It was a wonderful reminder
That Christ was born on Christmas day.

But sadly, things have changed;
An X has been substituted for Christ's name;
When Christ is removed from Christmas
The holiday won't be the same.

Christmas is forever, not just one day,
For loving, sharing, giving, are not to put away
Like bells and lights and tinsel, in some box upon a shelf.
The good you do for others is good you do yourself....
Norman Wesley Brooks (*Let Every day be Christmas, 1976).*

MY CHRISTMAS PRAYER

Dear gracious Father in heaven:
Thank you for the health to enjoy this day.
Thank you for my family and their love.
Father, we may not know the exact date
Our Savior was born, but we do know
That He was born—your gift to us.
Loving Father, help us to not only remember
The birth of our Savior, but His sacrifice
In death on the cross for our redemption.
Give us wisdom, courage and love to
Take the Good News message of Your
Love to a world that knows it not. May
The spirit of this holiday season always be
Remembered and shared the next 356 days.
In Jesus' name. Amen.

What is your Christmas Prayer?

CHRISTMAS: *The day into which we try*
To crowd all "the long arrears of
Kindness and humility of the whole year."
David Grayson

CHRISTMAS: *Christmas is celebrated*
The world over, but sadly, millions who celebrate
The day are ignorant of its meaning.
Author Unknown

AROMA OF COOKIES

The aroma filled the air,
The smell of special treats;
As Mama baked the cookies
For all of us to eat.

They were not as fancy
As those sold in the local store;
But the taste was so delicious;
You wanted to eat more and more.

When you added a glass of milk
To wash down your cookie treat;
You had a taste of heaven
That store bought couldn't beat.

It is not the gift, but the thought that counts.
                                          Henry Van Dyke

Christmas is not a time or a season
But state of mind. To cherish peace and good will,
To be plenteous in mercy, is to have
The real spirit of Christmas.
                                          Calvin Coolidge

He who has no Christmas in his heart,
Will find no Christmas under a tree.
                                          Charlotte Carpenter

SHARING YOUR MEMORIES OF CHRISTMAS

I have taken a few minutes to share some of my memories and beliefs about Christmas; now it is your turn. This is a wonderful exercise in a family and friend setting. Take a few minutes and respond to the following questions:

What is your favorite memory of Christmas?

What do you (did you) like most about Christmas?

What is your favorite Christmas song?

What is your favorite Christmas food?

What gift do you remember the most from Christmas?

What do you think makes a beautifully decorated tree?

What is your favorite memory of Santa Claus?

39

How/when do you do your Christmas shopping?

What is your favorite memory of a Christmas trip?

What was your biggest disappointment on a Christmas?

What is your favorite Christmas dessert?

What is your favorite Christmas movie?

What is your favorite written Christmas story?

What does the birth of Jesus mean to you?

THE BIRTH OF JESUS CHRIST

THE BIBLE ACCOUNT:

This is how the birth of Jesus Christ came about:
His mother Mary was pledged to be married
To Joseph, but before they came together, she
As found to be with child through the Holy Spirit. Because
Joseph her husband was a righteous man and did not
Want to expose her to public disgrace, he had in mind
To divorce her quietly. But after he had considered this,
An angel if the Lord appeared to him in a dream and
Said, 'Joseph son of David, do not be afraid to take Mary
Home as your wife, because what is conceived in her is
From the Holy Spirit. She will give birth to a son, and
You are to give him the name Jesus, because he will save
His people from their sins. All this took place to fulfill what
The Lord had said through the prophet: 'The virgin
Will be with child and will give birth to a son, and they
Will call him Immanuel'—which means, 'God with us.'
When Joseph woke up, he did what the angel of the Lord
Had commanded him and took Mary home as his wife.
But he had no union with her until she gave birth to a son.
And he gave him the name Jesus (**Matthew 1:18-24, NIV**).

RIDDLES ON CHRISTMAS

Q: What is red and white and black all over?
A: Santa Claus after he slid down the chimney.

Q: Why was Cinderella no good at football?
A: Her coach was a pumpkin.

Q: Why do reindeers scratch themselves?
A: Because they're the only ones who know where they itch.

Q: Why was Santa's little helper depressed?
A: Because he had low 'elf esteem.

Q: How does a snowman travel abroad?
A: By riding an icicle.

Q: Where do snow-women like to dance?
A: At snowballs.

Q: Why did the man get the sack from the orange juice factory?
A: Because he couldn't concentrate.

Q: What happens when kids eat the Christmas decorations?
A: They come down with tensel-itis.

Q: What do you call persons who are afraid of Santa Claus?
A: Claustrophobics.

Q: What do you get when you team Santa with a detective?
A: Santa Clues!

We hear the beating of wings over Bethlehem and a light that is not of the sun or of the stars shines in the midnight sky. Let the beauty of the story take away all narrowness, all thought of formal creeds. Let it be remembered as a story that has happened again and again, to men of many different races, that has been expressed through many religions, that has been called by many different names. Time and space and language lay no limitations upon human brotherhood. *(New York Times,* 25 December 1937, quoted in *Quotations for Special Occasions* by Maud van Buren, 1938, published by The H.W. Wilson Company, New York).

CHRISTMAS PAST

Each Christmas I remember
The ones of a long ago;
I see our mantelpiece adorned
With stockings in a row.

Each Christmas finds me dreaming
Of days that used to be,
When we hid presents here and there
For all of our family.

Each Christmas I remember
The fragrance in the air,
Of roasting turkey and pumpkin pies
And sweet cookies everywhere.

Each Christmas find me longing
For Christmases now past
And I am back in my childhood
As long as memories last.

Carice Williams

MY PERSONAL WISH FOR EVERYONE:

Take a few minutes and reflect on your wish for your family, friends, associates and the world at this Christmas season, and write it here:

_____

_____

_____

_____

_____

_____

_____

_____

_____

_____

_____

_____

_____

_____

_____

_____

Christmas! The very thought brings joy to our hearts.
No matter how we may dread the rush;
The long Christmas lists for gifts and cards
To be bought and given—when Christmas Day
Comes there is still the same warm feeling we had
As children, the same warmth that
Enfolds our hearts and our homes.

Joan Winmill Brown

To the American People: Christmas is not a time or a season but a state of mind. To cherish peace and good will, to be plenteous in mercy, is to have the real spirit of Christmas. If we think on these things, there will be born in us a Savior and over us will shine a star sending its gleam of hope to the world.
--Calvin Coolidge (1872-1933) American President.
Presidential message (December 25, 19:27).

Christmas—that magic blanket that wraps
Itself about us, that something so intangible
That it is like a fragrance. It may weave a spell of
Nostalgia. Christmas may be a day of feasting,
Or of prayer, but always it will be a day of
Remembrance—a day in which we think
Of everything we have ever loved.
---Augusta E. Rundell

*Remember, if Christmas isn't
Found in your heart,
You won't find it under a tree.*
Charlotte Carpenter

Which Christmas is the most
Vivid to me? It's always the
Next Christmas.
--*Joanne Woodward*

Printed in Great Britain
by Amazon